EARLY ENGLISH RECIPES

Selected from

𝕿𝖍𝖊 𝕳𝖆𝖗𝖑𝖊𝖎𝖆𝖓 𝕸𝖘. 279

of about 1430 *A.D.*

WITH WOOD ENGRAVINGS
BY
MARGARET WEBB

AND AN INTRODUCTION
BY
SIR STEPHEN GASELEE

CAMBRIDGE
AT THE UNIVERSITY PRESS
1937

CAMBRIDGE
UNIVERSITY PRESS

University Printing House, Cambridge CB2 8BS, United Kingdom

Cambridge University Press is part of the University of Cambridge.

It furthers the University's mission by disseminating knowledge in the pursuit of education, learning and research at the highest international levels of excellence.

www.cambridge.org
Information on this title: www.cambridge.org/9781107586406

© Cambridge University Press 1937

First published 1937
First paperback edition 2015

A catalogue record for this publication is available from the British Library

ISBN 978-1-107-58640-6 Paperback

PREFACE

In these recipes a few modern words have been substituted and occasional alterations have been made in the spelling and punctuation, for the sake of clearness. The text used is from the first of 'Two Fifteenth-Century Cookery-Books', edited by Thomas Austin and published in 1888 for the Early English Text Society, to whom an acknowledgment is gladly given. To the many friends who have helped me, particularly Mr Robert Gibbings and Mr F. Young, I offer my sincere thanks.

M. J. W.

18 *September* 1937

INTRODUCTION

When we read accounts of Old English meals, we are generally astonished at the amount of food consumed, and the multiplicity of the dishes: we often forget that there were several "services" simultaneously, not all consumed by each guest. We have very little idea how the various *plats* were prepared, and perhaps have an idea that our ancestors always cooked in the plain or "chop-house" style.

For this reason I find Miss Webb's little collection very welcome. The recipes are careful and detailed, and not above the intelligence of the ordinary housewife, though she may occasionally simplify a little; and I conceive that some of them will prove very delicious. As we all eat too much meat, I am particularly pleased to see a good many Friday and Lenten dishes of fish or eggs.

The number of spices, homely and foreign, is to be noted: it should be remembered that before the days of

2   cow-cake and "winter feeding", cattle had to be killed off in the autumn and the meat somehow kept until the next spring, and without plentiful spice it was hardly tolerable to the nose or palate. Hence the economic (and so political) importance of the Far Eastern spice islands.

But this is a side issue: and I will conclude by saying that I hope everyone else will enjoy this little book, both to read and practically, as much as I have.

STEPHEN GASELEE

11 *October* 1937

EARLY ENGLISH
RECIPES

COKYNTRYCE

Take a Capoun, and skald hym, and draw hem clene, and smyte hem a-to in the waste across; take a Pigge, and skald hym, and draw hym in the same maner, and smyte hem also in the waste; take a nedyl and a threde, and sewe the fore partye of the Capoun to the After parti of the Pygge; and the fore partye of the Pigge to the hynder party of the Capoun, & than stuffe hem as thou stuffyst a Pigge; putte hem on a spete, and Roste hym: and whan he is y-now, gild hem with yolkys of Eyroun, and pouder Gyngere and Safroun, thenne wyth the Jus of Percely withowte; and than serve it forth for a ryal mete.

EYROUN: *eggs.*

TENCHE IN SAWCE

Take a tenche whan he is boylid, & ley him on a dysshe; take Percely & Oynonys, & mynce hem to-ged-erys; take pouder Pepir, & Cinna-mon, & strew ther-on; take Vynegre, an caste Safroun ther-on, an coloure it, an serve it forth thanne alle colde.

A GOOS IN HOGEPOTTE

Take a Goos, & make hure clene,
& hacke hyre to gobettys, & put yn
a potte, and Water to, & seethe to-
gederys; than take Pepir & Burnt
brede, or Blode y-boylyd, & grynd
to-gederys Gyngere & Galyngale, &
temper uppe with Ale, & putte it ther-
to; & mynce Oynonys, & frye hem
in freysshe grece, & do ther-to a
porcyon of Wyne.

GALYNGALE: *English galingale, aromatic root of the rush Cypress. Galangale; tropical herb with fleshy, ginger-flavoured rhizomes.*

GYNGERBREDE

Take a quart of hony, & seethe it,
and skeme it clene; take Safroun,
pouder Pepir, & throw ther-on; take
gratyd Brede, & make it so stiff that
it wol be cut into strips; then take
pouder Cinnamon, & strew ther-on
y-now; then make yt square, lyke as
thou wolt slice yt; take when thou
slicest hyt, an caste Box leves above
y-stykyd ther-on on cloves. And if
thou wolt have it Red, coloure it with
Saunderys y-now.

SAUNDERYS: *Saunders wood; red sandal wood.*

Take smale byrdys, an pulle hem an drawe hem clene, an washe hem fayre, an schoppe of the leggys, and frye hem in a panne of freysshe grece ryt wyl; than ley hem on a fayre lynen clothe, an lette the grece renne owt; than take oynonys, an mynce hem smale, an frye hem on fayre freysshe grece, an caste hem on an erthen potte; than take a gode porcyon of cinnamon, an wyne, an draw thorw a straynoure, an caste in-to the potte with the oynonys; than caste the bryddys ther-to, an cloves, an maces, an a lytil quantyte of powder pepir ther-to, an lete hem boyle to-gederys y-now; than caste ther-to whyte sugre, an powder gyngere, salt, safron, an serve it forth.

BLAUNDYSORYE

Take Almaunde Mylke, an flowre of
Rys, & brawn of Capounys or of
hennys, & pouder Gyngere, & boyle
it to-gederys, & make it thick; an
whan thou dressest yn, take Maces,
Quybibes, & caste a-bove, & serve
forth.

QUYBIBES: *Cubeb; tropical black pepper.
Piper Cubeba; climbing shrub from Java.*

POTROUS

Take a shovel of iron, and hete it
brennyng hote; & than take it owt of
the fyre, & fille it fulle of Salt; than
make a pitte in the Salt al holow, the
shape of a treen dyssche; & sette the
panne & the Salt over the fyre a-gen,
tyl the Salt be brennyng hote; & than
caste the white & the yolkys of Eyroun in-to the hole of the Salte, &
lat seethe over the fyre tyl it be half
harde; & than put a dyssche half fulle
of Salt; and than take a dressoure
knyf, & put undernethe the Salt in
the panne, & heave it uppe so fayre,
that the cofyn with the Eyroun breke
not; than sette it on the dyssche wyth
the Salt, & than serve it forth.

TREEN: *treen bolle; wooden bowl.*

Take Elys or Gurnard, & parte hem, half in Wyne & half in watere, in-to a potte; take Percely and Oynonys & hewe hem smalle; take Cloves or Maces and caste ther-on; take Saf-roun, and caste ther-to, and sette on the fyre, & let boyle tylle it be y-now; then sette it a-doun; take poudere Gyngere, Cinnamon, Galingale, and temper it uppe with Wyne, and cast on the potte and serve forth.

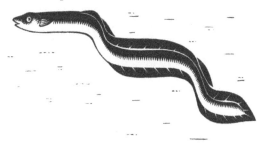

SORE SENGLE: *soré; reeked or made red as with saffron.* "*Soringue: Eele sauce made of fried Onions, and toas-bread steeped in Pease broth, then strayned with wine, vinegar, Cinnamon, Ginger, and other spices, all put into a pot with the Eeles cut into peeces, and (after a little season-ing with saffron and salt) throughly boyled.*"
COTGRAVE, 'French Dict.' (1611).

POKEROUNCE

Take Hony, & caste it in a potte tyl it wexe thick y-now; take & skeme it clene. Take Gyngere, Cinnamon and Galyngale, & caste ther-to; take whyte Brede, & kytte to big slices, & toste hem; take the paste whyle it is hot, & sprede it uppe-on the slices with a spone, & plante it with Pynes, & serve forth.

PYNES: *whole pepper, or seeds of fir cones.*

PETY PERNOLLYS

Take fayre Floure, Safroun, Sugre, & Salt, & make ther-of past; than make smal cofyns; then take yolkys of Ey-roun, & separate hem fro the whyte; & lat the yolkys be al hole, & not to-broke, & ley iii or iv yolkys in a cofyn; and than take marow of bonys, ii or iii gobettys, & cowche in the cofynn; than take pouder Gyngere, Sugre, Raysonys, & caste a-bove; & than cover the cofyn with the same past, & bake hem, & frye hem in fayre grece, & serve forth.

COFYN: *crust of a pie.*

Take Chyryis, & pike out the stonys,
waysshe hem clene in wyne, than
wryng hem thorw a clothe, & do it
on a potte, & put ther-to whyte grece
a quantyte, & a partye of Floure of
Rys, & make it thick; do ther-to
hwyte Hony or Sugre, make it piquant
with Venegre; season it with stronge
pouder of Cinnamon & of Galyngale,
& allay it with a grete porcyoun of
yolkys of Eyroun; coloure it with Safroun   or Saunderys; & whan
thou   servyste in, plante it
with   Chyrioun, & serve
forth.

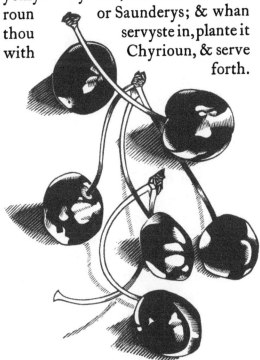

HENNYS IN GAUNCELYE

Take Hennys, an roste hem; take
Mylke an Garleke, an grynd it, an do
it in a panne, an hewe the hennys
ther-on with yolkys of eyron, an
coloure it with Safroun an Mylke,
an serve forth.

GAYLEDE

Take Almaunde Mylke & flowre of
Rys, & do ther-to Sugre or Hony, &
Powder Gyngere & Galyngale; then
take figys, an kerve hem a-to, or Raysonys unstoned, or hard Wastel y-
dicyd and coloure it with Saunderys,
& seethe it & dresse hem yn.

WASTEL: *Wastel bread; bread made of fine
flour.*

CRUSTE ROLLE

Take fayre smal Flowre of whete;
take Eyroun & breke ther-to, &
coloure the past with Safroun; rolle it
on a borde also thinne as parchement,
rounde a-bowte as an oblye; frye
hem, & serve forth; and thus may
do in lente, but do away the Eyroun,
& take mylke of Almaundys, & frye
hem in Oyle, & then serve forth.

OBLYE: *sacramental wafer.*

Take and make litel cofyns, and take
Chykonys boylid; or Porke boylid
and smale y-hackyd; or of hem
bothe: take Cloves, Maces, Quybibes,
and hakke with-alle, and mingle yt
with crumbled Marow & lay on Sugre
y-now; than ley it on the cofynne,
and in the myddel lay a gobet of
marow, & Sugre round a-boute y-
now, and lat   bake; and
this is for
soperys.

OYSTRYS IN GRAVY BASTARD

Take grete Oystrys, an schale hem; an take the water of the Oystrys, & ale, an brede y-straynid, an the water also, an put it on a potte, an Gyngere, Sugre, Saffron, powder pepir, and Salt, an let it boyle wyl; then put yn the Oystrys ther-to, and dresse it forth.

BASTARD: *a sweet Spanish wine.*

WALKYS IN BRUETTE

Take Walkys an seethe in Ale, then pyke hem clene; than wasshem in Water an Salt be hem-self, and fyrst wyth Ale & Salt, and do so whele they ben slippery; then putte hem in Vynegre, an ley Perceli a-bove, an serve ynne.

WALKYS: *whelks.*

BRUETTE or BRWT: *Brouet;* "*Potage, or broth; also, any liquor, podge, or sauce, of the thicknesse, or consistence of that whereof our pruine-tarts are made.*" COTGRAVE.

Take gode almaunde mylke y-draw wyth wyn, an let hem boyle togederys, an caste ther-to Safroun an Salt; an than take Paynemayn, an kytte it an toste it, an wete it in wyne, an ley it on a dysshe, an caste the syrip ther-on. And than make a dredge of powder Gyngere, Sugre, cinnamon, Cloves, Maces, an caste ther-on When it is y-dressid, an serve thanne forth for a potage gode.

PAYNEMAYN: *Pain Manchet; Manchet refers to the short curtailed character of Roll bread.*

A POTAGE ON A FYSDAYE

Take an seethe ii or iii Applys y-parede, & strayne hem thorw a straynoure, & Flowre of Rys ther-with; than take whyte Wyne, & strayne it with-alle; than loke that it be nowt y-bounde to moche with the Floure of Rys, than if it a-boyle; then caste ther-to Saunderys & Saf-roun, & loke it be marbylle; than take Raysonys, and caste ther-on, & Al-maundys y-schredyd ther-on y-nowe; & mynce Datys Smale & caste ther-on, & a lytil Hony to make it dulcet, or ellys Sugre; thenne caste ther-to Maces & Cloves, Pepir, Cinnamon, Gyngere, & other spycery y-now; then take Peres, & seethe hem a lytil; then heat hem on the colys tyl they ben tendyr; than smale shred hem rounde; & a lytil before thou serve it in, throw hem on the potage, & so serve hem in almost flatte, not fully.

TANNYE

Take almaunde Mylke, & Sugre, an powdere Gyngere, & of Galyngale, & of Cinnamon, & Rede Wyne, & boyle to-gederys; & that is gode tannye.

Take Flowrys of Hawthorn, boyle
hem, presse hem, bray hem smal,
temper hem uppe with Almaunde
mylke, or gode Cowe Mylke, allay
it with Amydoun or Flowre of Rys;
take Sugre y-now, an putte ther-to,
or hony in defaute; coloure it with
the same that the flowrys be on y-
peyntid a-bove.

AMYDOUN: *wheat flour, steeped, strained,
and dried in the sun.*

JUSCHELLE of FYSSHE

Take fayre Roe of Pyke, & caste it raw on a morter, an caste ther-to gratid brede, an bray hem as smale as thow mayste; & if it be to styf, caste ther-to Almaunde mylke, an bray hem to-gederys, an stere it to-gederys, & caste ther-to a littel Safroun & Salt, an whyte Sugre, an putte al in a fayre Treen bolle, & rub it to-gederys wyth the hond, an loke that it be not to thick, but as a man may pore it out of the bolle; & than take a Chafoure or a panne, an caste ther-in fayre gravey of pyke or of Freysshe Samoun, y-draw thorw a straynoure, & sette it on the fyre; thanne take fayre Percely an Sage, an caste ther-to, an lat it boyle, an caste ther-to a lytil Safroun an Salt; & whan it hath y-boylid a whyle, stere it faste, an caste the Stuffe ther-to, an stere it evermore; an whan alle is oute of the bolle, caste a litel an a litel in-to the chafoure, or the panne; stere it soffter an soffter, tylle it come to-gedere; than gader it to-gederys with a ladelle or a Sky-moure, softe, tille it be round to-gedere; thanne take it fro the fyre, an sette the vesselle on a fewe colys,

& late it wexe styf be hys owne
acord; than serve forth.

CHAFOURE: *for heating; (chauffer).*

CRYSPEY

Take Whyte of Eyroun, Mylke, and
Floure, and a lytel Barm, and bete it
to-gederys, and draw it thorw a straynoure, so that it be renneng, and
not to styf, and caste Sugre ther-to,
and Salt; thanne take a chafer ful of
freysshe grece boyling, and put the
hond in the Bature, and lat the bature
renne dowun by the fyngerys into the
chafere; and whan it is ronne to-
gedere on the
chafere, and
is y-now,
take a

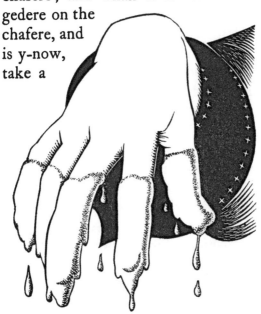

skymer, and take it up, and lat al the grece renne owt, and put it on a fayre dyssche, and cast ther-on Sugre y-now, and serve forth.

LAMPRAYS BAKE

Take & make fayre round cofyns of fyne past, & take Freysschelampreys, & late hem blode, iii fyngerys within the tayle, & lat hem blede in a vesselle, & late hym deye in the same vesselle in the same blode; than take broun Brede, & kyt it, & stepe it in the Venegre, & draw thorw a straynoure; than take the same blode, & pouder of Cinnamon, & cast ther-to tyl it be broun; than caste ther-to pouder Pepir, Salt, & Wyne a lytelle, that it be not to strong of venegre. An skald the Lampray, & pare hem clene, & couche hym round on the cofyn, tyl he be covered; than cover hym fayre with a lede, save a lytel hole in the myddelle, & at that hole, blow in the cofynne with the mowthe a gode blast of Wynde. And sodenly stoppe the hole, that the wynd a-byde with-ynne, to reyse uppe the cofynne that he falle nowt a-dowune; & whan he is a lytel y-hardid in the oven, pryke the cofyn with a pynne y-stekyd on a roddys ende, for brekyng of the cofynne, & than lat bake, & serve forth colde. And when the lamprey is take owt of the cofynne & etyn, take the Syrippe in the cofynne, & put on a chargere, & caste Wyne ther-to, an pouder Gyngere, & lat boyle in the fyre. Than take fayre Paynemayn y-wette in Wyne, & ley the soppis in the cofynne of the lamprey, & ley the Syrippe a-bove, & ete it so hot; for it is gode lordys mete.

STORION IN BROTHE

Take fayre Freysshe Storgeoun, an choppe it in fayre water; thanne take

it fro the fyre, an strayne the brothe thorw a straynoure in-to a potte, an pyke clene the Fysshe, an caste ther-to powder Pepir, Cloves, Maces, Cinnamon; & thanne take fayre Brede, and stepe it in the same lycowre, & caste ther-to, an let boyle to-gederys, & caste then Safroun ther-to, Gyngere, an Salt, & Vynegre, & thanne serve it forth ynne.

MAMMENYE BASTARDE

Take a potelle of Clarifiyd Hony, & a pounde of Pynys, & a pounde Raysonys, & a pound of Saunderys, and pouder Cinnamon, & ii galouns of Wyne or Ale, & a pound of Pepir, & caste alle on a potte, & skym yt; than take iii pounde of Amyndouns, & a galon of Wyne, & a gode galon of Venegre, & let stepe up to-gederys, & draw thorw a straynoure; an whan the potte boylith, caste the lycoure ther-to, an lat it be alle styf; than take pouder Gyngere, Salt & Safron, an sesyn it uppe, an serve alle flat on a dysshe, all hote, an caste pouder Gyngere ther-on, an serve forth.

Take Molberys, and wrynge a gode hepe of hem thorw a clothe; take Vele, hew it and grynd it smal, and caste ther-to; take gode Spicery an Sugre, and caste ther-to; take Wastil-brede and grate it, and yolkys of Eyroun, and allay it uppe ther-with, and caste gode pouder of Spycery ther-an above; and than serve it forth.

APPRAYLERE

Take the fleysshe of the lene Porke,
& seethe it wel: & whan it is boylid, hew it smal; take than Safroun,
Gyngere, Cinnamon, Salt, Galyngale,
old chese, crumbed Brede, & bray it
smal on a morter; caste the fleysshe
in to the spicery, & loke that it
be wil y-ground, & temper it uppe
with raw Eyroun; than take a longe
Pitcher, al round over alle it should
be rinsed; than cast out the grece, &
fulle the Pitcher of the stuffing,
& take a pese of fayre Cannevas, &
doble it as moche as thou may cover
the mouthe with-al, & bynd it fast
a-bowte the rim, & caste hym to
seethe with the grete Fleysshe, in lead
or in Caldron, for it be wyl sodden;
take then uppe the Pitcher, & breke
it, an save the stuffing; & have a fayre
spit, & broach it thorw, & lay it to the
fyre; & than have a gode Bature of
Spicerye, Safroun, Galyngale, Cinnamon, & ther-of y-now, & flowre, &
grynd smal in a morter, & temper it
up with raw Eyroun, & do ther-to
Sugre of Alexandria y-now; & ever
as it dryeth, baste it with bature, &
sette forth in servyce.

APPRAYLERE: *appareillé*; *dressed, seasoned.*

Take gode Wyne, an gode pouder, and
Brede y-ground, an sugre, an boyle
it to-gederys; than take Trowtys,
Rochys, Perchys, or Carpys, or alle
these to-gederys, an make hem clene,
and aftere roste hem on a Grydelle;
than hewe hem in gobettys: whan
they ben boylid, fry hem in oyle a
lytil, then caste in the brwet; & whan
thou dressist it, take Maces, Cloves,
Quybibes, Gilliflowers, an cast a-bove,
and serve forth.

VENYSON WITH FURMENTY

Take whete and pyke it clene, and do it in a morter, an caste a lytel water ther-on; an stampe with a pestel tyl it loses the husks; than blow owt the husks, an put it in a potte, an let seethe tyl it breke; than set yt douun, an sone after set it over the fyre, an stere it wyl; an whan thow hast boy-lid it wyl, put ther-inne swete mylke, an seethe it to-gederys, an stere it wyl; and whan it is y-now, coloure it wyth safron, an salt it evenly, and dresse it forth, and the venyson in a-nother dyshe with fayre hot water.

HANONEY

Take an draw the Whyte & the yolkys of the Eyroun thorw a stray-noure; than take Oynonys, & shred hem smal; than take fayre Boter or grece, & scarcely cover the panne ther-with, an frye the Oynonys, & than caste the Eyroun in the panne, & breke the Eyrouns & the Oynonys to-gederys; an than lat hem frye to-gederys a litel whyle; than take hem up, an serve forth alle to-broke to-gederys on a fayre dyssche.

WITH-OWT FYRE

Take fowre pounde of Almaundys, and ley in Water over hem, an blanche hem, & on the morwe grynd hem ryth wyl, an draw ther-of a thicke mylke; than take Rys, and wasshem clene, an grynd hem wyl, & draw hem uppe wyth the Mylke thorw a straynoure, an do it on a bolle, & parte it in the vesselle, an do in al whyte Sugre, an every vesselle Cloves, Maces, Quybibes, & pouder Cinnamon; & let that one party ben whyte, that other yelow, & that other grene with Percely; And ley of every a strip in a dysshe, an loke that Mylke be temperyd wyth wyne, an that other with Rede wyn.

TALBOTTYS

Take an Hare, an fle hem clene; then
take the blode, & Brede, an Spycery,
an grynde to-gederys, & draw it uppe
with the brothe; than take Wyne or
Ale, an cast ther-to, & make gobettys,
& thanne serve it forth.

YRCHOUNS

Take Piggis stomachs, & skalde hem
wel; take groundyn Porke, & knede
it with Spicerye, with pouder Gyngere, & Salt & Sugre; put it in the
stomach, but fille it nowt to fulle;
then sewe hem with a fayre threde,
& putte hem in a Spete as men don
piggys; take blaunchid Almaundys,
& kerf hem long, smal and scharpe,
& frye hem in grece and sugre; take
a litel prycke, & prykke the yrchouns,
an putte in the holes the Almaundys,
every hole half, & eche fro other;
ley hem then to the fyre; when they
ben rostid, glaze hem, sum wyth
Whete Flowre & mylke of Almaundys, sum grene, sum blake with
Blode, & lat hem nowt browne to
moche, & serve forth.

YRCHOUNS: *urchins; hedgehogs, so called
from being bristly with almonds.*

Take fayre buttocks of Vele & hewe
hem, and grynd hem in a morter, &
wyth the yolkys of eyroun, & with
the whyte of eyroun; an caste ther-to
powder Pepyr, Cinnamon, Gyngere,
Cloves powder, and datys y-mynced,
Safroun, & raysonys, an seethe in a
panne wyth fayre water, an let it boyle;
than wete the handys in Raw eyroun,
than take it an rolle it in the hondys,
smaller or gretter, as thow wolt have
it, an caste it in-to
boyling water, an
let boyle y-now;

than putte it on a Spete round, an lete hem rosty; then take flowre, an yolkys of eyroun an the whyte, an draw hem thorwe a straynowre, an caste ther-to pouder Gyngere, an make the bature grene with the Jus of Percely, or Mallows, in tyme of yere Whete, an caste on the pommys as they turne a-boute, & serve forth.

VYAUND LECHE

Take Eyroun, the whyte & the yolke, & caste hem in a morter, an breke hem wyl; than take cowe mylke & caste ther-to, & mingle hem wyl to-gederys; than put al in a panne, & lat boyle; & with ale make it to a posset; then hange the curds on a pynne, & let it over-renne; mingle the curds with hony; then take the bladys of Barlyche, or of Percely, & stampe hem, & wrynge thorw a clothe; & so alle the grene mingle it a-mong the curds; thenne take the curds that comen fro the dairy-maid, mingle hem to-gederys, presse hem, & serve hem forth; an the coloure wyl ben than Motley.

Take the Blode of hym, & the grece
of hymself, & Otemele, & Salt, &
Pepir & Gyngere, & mingle these to-
gederys wel, & than putte this in the
Gutte of the purpays, & than lat it
seethe esyli, & not hard, a good whylys;
& than take hym uppe, & broyle
hym a lytil, &
than serve forth.

Take Rys, an bray hem wyl, & temper
hem with Almaunde mylke, & boyle
it; & take Applys, & pare hem, an
smal shred hem in mossellys; throw
on sugre y-now, and coloure it with
Safroun, & caste ther-to gode pouder,
& serve forth.

NOTEYE

Take a gret porcyoun of Haselle
levys, & grynd in a morter as smal
as thou may, whyl that they ben
yonge; take than, & draw uppe a
not too strong Mylke of Almaundys
y-blaunchyd, and temper it with
Freysshe brothe; wryng out clene
the Jus of the levys; take Fleysshe
of Porke or of Capoun, and grynd
it smal, & temper it uppe with the
mylke, & caste it in a potte, & the
Jus ther-to, do it over the fyre & late
it boyle; take flour of Rys, & allay
it; take & caste Sugre y-now ther-
to, & Vynegre a quantyte, & pouder
Gyngere, & Safroun it wel, & Salt;
take smal nuts, & breke hem; take
the kyrnellys, & make hem whyte,
& frye hem uppe in grece; plante
ther-with the mete & serve forth.

Take Eyroun, & blow owt that ys
with-ynne atte other ende; than
waysshe the schulle clene in warme
water; than take gode mylke of
Almaundys, & sette it on the fyre;
than take a fayre canvas, & pore the
mylke ther-on, & lat renne owt the
water; then take it owt on the clothe,
& gader it to-gedere with a platere;
then putte sugre y-now ther-to; than
take a part, & colour it with Safroun
a lytil, & do ther-to pouder Cinnamon; than take & put of the whyte
in the nether ende of the schulle,
& in the myddel the yolk, & fylle it
uppe with the whyte, but not to fulle
for goyng over; than sette it in the
fyre and roste it, and serve forth.

www.ingramcontent.com/pod-product-compliance
Ingram Content Group UK Ltd.
Pitfield, Milton Keynes, MK11 3LW, UK
UKHW042149280225
455719UK00001B/216

9 781107 586406